GABRIEL LADERMAN

Unconventional
Realist

GUEST CURATORS

DAVID CARBONE

LINCOLN PERRY

LANGDON QUIN

University of Virginia Art Museum
Museum of Art, University of New Hampshire

This catalogue accompanies an exhibition coorganized by the
University of Virginia Art Museum and the Museum of Art,
University of New Hampshire.

The catalogue was edited by Carrie Sherman and designed
by Valerie Lester, Office of Editorial and Creative Services,
University of New Hampshire.

Library of Congress Control Number: 2008926406

ISBN: 978-0-9648953-6-2

EXHIBITION TOUR

UNIVERSITY OF VIRGINIA ART MUSEUM
Charlottesville, Virginia
August 15–October 12, 2008

MUSEUM OF ART, UNIVERSITY OF NEW HAMPSHIRE
Durham, New Hampshire
November 1–December 15, 2008

ROSEMARY BERKEL AND HARRY L. CRISP II MUSEUM
Southeast Missouri State University
Cape Girardeau, Missouri
January 23–March 15, 2009

NEW YORK ACADEMY OF ART
New York, New York
March 31–April 28, 2009

LOUISIANA STATE UNIVERSITY MUSEUM OF ART
Baton Rouge, Louisiana
September 4–October 25, 2009

LENDERS TO THE EXHIBITION

Catholic Diocese of Baton Rouge

Malcolm Holzman

Innes Collection

Gabriel Laderman

Dr. and Mrs. Edmund Pillsbury

The Spurzem Family Collection

CONTENTS

ACKNOWLEDGMENTS

Collaboration enhances any project, bringing more depth, a wider reach, and greater rewards. Both the University of Virginia Art Museum and the Museum of Art at the University of New Hampshire have benefited from our partnership to produce an exhibition and catalogue that pays tribute to the artist Gabriel Laderman. Laderman's contributions to the twentieth-century resurgence of figurative painting in America—both as a painter and an educator—have been far reaching. His influence is amplified through the work and teaching of those who studied painting with him—among them the three curators of this exhibition: David Carbone, Lincoln Perry, and Langdon Quin. Recognizing Laderman's influence on their lives as artists and teachers, they have been committed to the project—in all its details—since its inception.

We are grateful to all three of the curators for their collective efforts. Determined to shape an exhibition that represents the range of Laderman's work throughout four decades, the curators rolled up their sleeves and combed through three storage facilities to select the best works still in the artist's possession and identified key works to be borrowed from private collections. All three were extremely helpful in locating other institutions interested in hosting the exhibition. Individually, the curators made distinct contributions to the project. David Carbone graciously undertook much of the time-consuming and exacting work of providing details about the paintings for the loan negotiation and catalogue and coordinated many details with the artist and the staff at the University of Virginia Art Museum. His essay for this catalogue provides an excellent, yet concise, overview of the development of Laderman's work and its general concerns. As an adviser and reviewer, he also made significant contributions to the content and development of the major catalogue essay by Lincoln Perry. Perry's insightful essay, written from the perspective of a painter and educator, brings us closer to the artist, his work, and his writing. Perry also contacted numerous museums to secure their interest in hosting the exhibition and served as a curatorial liaison to the University of Virginia Art Museum. Langdon Quin facilitated communications among the curators and contributed to both the fund-raising efforts and photography arrangements for the catalogue. His introduction to this catalogue captures the profound way in which Gabriel Laderman influenced the three curators as painters and teachers.

The University of Virginia Art Museum managed the tasks of negotiating the loans and arranging for the packing and shipping of the works for the exhibition. We wish to acknowledge the museum's former director, Jill Hartz, for her early support of the collaboration, as well as the important contributions of Andrea Douglas, curator of collections and exhibitions, Ana Marie Liddell, exhibitions coordinator, and Jean Collier, collections manager. The Museum of Art at the University of New Hampshire coordinated the production of the exhibition catalogue and the arrangements for traveling the exhibition to three

ACKNOWLEDGMENTS

additional art institutions. In these efforts, the contributions made by Astrida Schaeffer, assistant director, Cindy Farrell, administrative assistant, and Catherine A. Mazur, education and publicity coordinator, have been invaluable. The work of an accomplished editor is often invisible to readers; while a designer's good work is self-evident in the look of a catalogue. This project has benefited greatly from the talents and expertise of Carrie Sherman, editor, and Valerie Lester, designer, both of the Office of Editorial and Creative Services at University of New Hampshire.

The opportunity to share this exhibition with three other fine art institutions is gratifying, and we extend our thanks to the following for their commitment to hosting the exhibition: Stanley Grand, director of the Rosemary Berkel and Harry L. Crisp II Museum at Southeast Missouri State University; John Jacobsmeyer, chair of faculty of the New York Academy of Art; and Thomas A. Livesay, executive director of the Louisiana State University Museum of Art. We appreciate the willingness of each of the lenders to share works from their collections, and all who see this exhibition will benefit from their generosity. Jane Schoelkopf, wife and partner of the late Robert Schoelkopf, whose gallery showed Gabriel Laderman's work for more than

two decades, supplied David Carbone with information used to locate collectors to secure several important loans. Her enthusiasm for this project and her unwavering belief in Laderman's work are warmly acknowledged.

We are most grateful to several individuals—Allison and Donald Innes, Ruth Cross, and Richard and Melissa Spurzem—as well as the Hackett-Freedman Gallery in San Francisco. Their ongoing interest in Laderman's work and generous support have made this exhibition possible. Its showing at the University of New Hampshire is supported in part by a grant from The FEDCO Charitable Foundation, a gift from Michael F. Ananian, and contributions from the Friends of the Museum of Art.

Elizabeth Hutton Turner
University Professor and Interim Director
University of Virginia Art Museum

and

Vicki C. Wright
Director
Museum of Art, University of New Hampshire

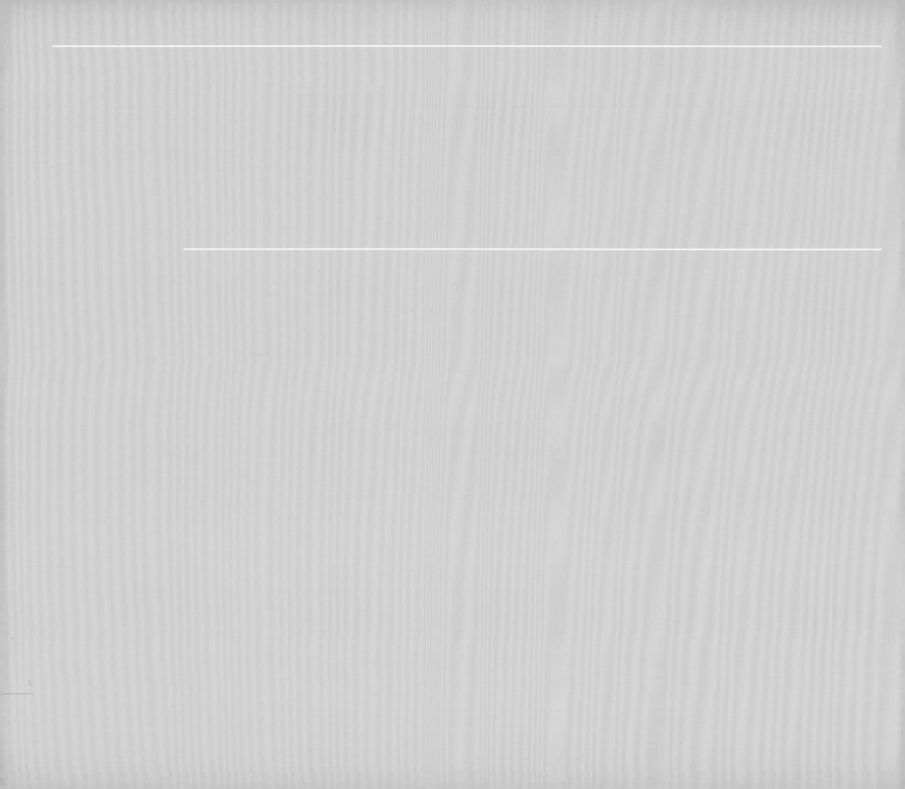

x

INTRODUCTION

Throughout my thirty years of working with art students, I have often thought of my teacher, Gabriel Laderman. He has been both an inspiring model and formidable artistic presence to me and to a whole generation of painters. In thinking about the quality of my earliest interactions with Gabriel, I know I join many of his past students who recall their daily "at easel" contact with him in a similar way: his blunt appraisal of our efforts could feel harsh. Over time, most of us realized that any gruffness was paired with specificity, cogency, and great generosity. Most importantly, if aspects of his criticism weren't immediately apprehensible, they would slowly reveal themselves as truths as the weeks, months, and even years wore on. This process of absorption could take place long after the close of a semester and long after the several minutes required of a student to pencil in a few small boxes on an end-of-term course evaluation form. To me, this is the mark of a truly great teacher of painting: the ability to articulate clearly a prescriptive address of a picture's particular problems and, at the same time, to connect its fullest comprehension to an unexplored realm that the student is challenged to investigate as time goes on.

The three curators involved in the organization of this show—myself, David Carbone, and Lincoln Perry—are all former students of Laderman. We are among countless others who studied with this remarkable painter and teacher in the early and mid-1970s in various contexts: David and myself in summer programs at Skowhegan and Tanglewood, respectively; others in art schools such as Pratt and the Art Students League, or in university M.F.A. graduate programs such as Yale, Brooklyn College, or in Lincoln's case, Queens College. Over the intervening years the three of us have each become artists and teachers ourselves and found both our work and pedagogy to have inexorably evolved from Gabriel's demanding example. And, we each have come to believe that the discrete and particular variants derived from our understanding of his ideas are what separate us while at the same time connect us and validate our use of them. We have each had other mentors, other pictorial ambitions, and made our own formulations about what it means to paint or teach. But what we are emphatically agreed upon (and this is the genesis of this show) is the urgency of assembling and presenting a representative body of Laderman's life's work. Our hope is that this exhibition will serve not only to trace the development of this unique artist's powerful vision, but also to make his importance to the course of late-twentieth-century American painting available to a new generation of viewers trying to make sense of painting's relevance to contemporary experience. Aside from my deepest appreciation and thanks to Gabriel, I wish to thank Carol Laderman, my co-curators David and Lincoln, and most especially Vicki Wright, director of the University of New Hampshire's Museum of Art, for her patience and tireless efforts in bringing this endeavor to fruition.

Langdon Quin
University of New Hampshire

AN UNCONVENTIONAL REALIST

Now that figuration has reentered the mainstream of contemporary art, Gabriel Laderman is being celebrated as one of the most challenging and outstanding painters of the last half century. Laderman is a key figure in the development of post-abstract figuration, or new realism, as it was called, during the 1960s and '70s. He became an early and important model as an artist, critic, and theorist for peers and younger painters, here and abroad. Laderman was one of the first painters to reject the conventions of abstract expressionism and collage. In its place, he brought the structural and metaphoric thinking of abstraction to perceptual representation. Standing apart from academic formulas, and from any obvious modernist strategy, he completely rethought figuration.

Laderman was able to draw on and reformulate metaphoric structures from multiple cultural sources—modernism and the early Renaissance, seventeenth-century realism and East Asian art, fusing them into new and contemporary works by experimenting with these ideas as he painted directly from nature. The result is a complex body of work which carries on a dialogue with past art. Just as Laderman's work is conditioned by our awareness of his use of the past, the art past is also changed in our understanding of his work. In this dialogue deeper readings are revealed that transform the idea of tradition in significant ways which have been famously elaborated on by Mikhail Bakhtin and T. S. Eliot. During the halcyon years of criticism in the pages of *ARTnews* and *Artforum,* Laderman's writing on figuration explored the potential for originality embedded within neglected aspects of various art traditions.

This exhibition examines four decades of his development as an artist, working with still life, landscape, portraiture, the nude, and narrative. In his early still lifes and landscapes, Laderman tackled the problems of creating paintings as spatial worlds rather than mere images. Emphasizing objectivity, this work suppressed emotional qualities in favor of a 1960s "cool." The quality of light, the visceral geometry of space in depth and as a pattern on the surface, the haunted metaphysical stillness, all contribute to a powerful feeling of fatality. This sensation of mortality runs throughout Laderman's works and suggests the urgent moral force of his work.

Landscapes by Laderman often depict urban American cities seen where mankind's efforts are implicitly set against nature's infinite expanse. Startling and fresh formulations of landscape forms are joined with modernist constructivist ideas to establish a symbolic pictorial dynamic. A factory, an office tower, or a cathedral creates vertical rhythmic intervals that play against the flutter of horizontal branches of foliage while roofs, bridges, and roads stretch back toward the distant horizon. The symbolic dynamic is felt in the pictorial tensions between these elements as they are made stark in the harsh vibration of light.

As his late style emerged, Laderman's work began to swing back and forth between unique hybrid forms; between a metaphysical-naturalist mode and a postcubist expressionism. With such varied works, Laderman was able to join the vehemence of his sensory perceptions to his chief dramatic subjects: death and desire. In precarious scenes of modern lovers, he moves us from unequal loves, to the emotional dwarfing of Oedipal desires, and beyond to Thanatos.

The intensity of these works has been underlined by the refraction of several tragic events: during World War II, Laderman's elder brother was brutally murdered by German peasants when he was forced to parachute from his plane; in the early eighties, Laderman and his wife were witnesses to a murder committed during a robbery; a few years later a model he was working closely with was killed and eaten by a madman; and his wife suffered a near fatal stroke. Laderman himself has lived, somewhat precariously, for more than two decades with leukemia.

There is an ethos in Laderman's work that resists "norms": classical, realist, photo, or pop. Instead of pursuing a sense of beauty or "good taste," Laderman has continuously sought to experiment with the means of representation. He gambles on the modernist strategy of the surprisingly ugly or awkward form to provide us with an awakening jolt to our expectations. In the vertigo of curving space, in the wrenching shifts of forms, and with disjunctive rhythmic movements, Laderman creates a pictorial syntax which mirrors reality not as we agree to see it, but as we feel or know it to be the moment we lose our step.

In his subtle blending of metaforms from twentieth-century abstraction, the art of Christian Europe, that of China and Japan, and even the animism of Malaysia, Laderman has enacted, through his synthesis of aesthetic and cultural enthusiasms, a distinct and subtle mindset. It is at once radical and conservative, secular and metaphysical, developing out of the expressive idealism of modernism and its Freudian inheritance. His recent, often complex, figure compositions are among the most challenging and rewarding works produced anywhere in the last quarter century. Here is a New York painter who has created out of diverse cultural involvements a distinctly American synthesis, one that expresses rare qualities in today's art: objectivity and meditation, empathy and compassion, delirium and dream.

David Carbone
University of Albany, State University of New York

GABRIEL LADERMAN: COOL AND HOT

THE CONTEXT

In New York's art world from the 1960s to the '80s, people seemed to either love or hate Gabriel Laderman. He could be so overpowering, his opinions so well informed and thought out, his delivery so articulate and often so loud that you couldn't just ignore him. Of course, his work spoke very clearly for itself, and still does. He appealed to those who were passionately interested in the breadth and depth of art, and deeply ambitious for art as an agent of change. And he was not a solitary figure. New York had become a hotbed not just for the art movements that were garnering most of the media attention, but for a group of powerfully vocal and dedicated advocates of a new figuration.

Starting in 1969, figurative artists would periodically meet at the Educational Alliance, a Jewish community organization founded in 1893 on the Lower East Side in Manhattan, where one could participate in shout-fests over issues an outsider might see as arcane, but which always had a moral correlative. It was as if political brawls about points of honor still haunted the Alliance's dusty, history-laden halls. When the larger-than-life personalities at these get-togethers took positions on such issues as the linear versus the painterly (which some had the good humor to call tight versus sloppy), one didn't see gentlemanly debates on Wölfflin's art historical categories. These were knock-down, drag-out fights, almost coming to blows. Linear versus painterly? Why not say moral clarity versus sentimentalized expressionism! No, on the contrary, we're talking about dutiful rendering versus emotional honesty! Picasso's neoclassical period? Work done in bad faith! No, it points the way out of the abstract woods! Aesthetics and ethics were somehow inseparable when it came to form making, color, pictorial depth, or narrative.

And though such lines were drawn on principle, powerful personalities were certainly involved. Aristodimos Kaldis, a self-proclaimed naif, arrived at the party like some Zorbatic Ancient Mariner, warning all against over-sophistication. Paul Georges and his beer-guzzling henchmen appropriated the macho muscle of abstract expressionism and distrusted too much ideation—perhaps even thought. Leland Bell had his own cohort and insisted the only acceptable thread of influence came through Derain to Balthus, Giacometti, and Helion, and any other path was unacceptable. Not just misguided, but unethical. Bell's magnetic eyes would bulge dangerously from their sockets as he fulminated like an angry god, even if his opponent was as elderly as Alice Neel. "Age makes no difference, Alice!!!" Bell roared one evening, towering over the aged Circe, while she continued knitting as if Bell were no more than a hovering fly. Neel loved getting under other people's skin. Any number of strong women attended. Some, like Rosemary Beck, happily joined the fray, breathing the testosterone-laden air, while others, like Louisa Matthiasdottir, radiated silent authority. Lennart Anderson was similarly reticent, distancing himself from the Sturm und Drang, for his was a diffident stance, both modest and arrogant. "I'm not so good," he would say, "but everyone else is worse."

Robert Rosenblum came to the Alliance to speak about an exhibition he curated at the Metropolitan Museum of Art, French Painting 1774–1830: The Age of Revolution. The premise of the show was that much more goes on in any historical period than is written into the record, and while his remarks should have given some of the more thuggish artists hope that their work might be resuscitated by such a show in the future, personal epithets were hurled at the urbane art historian. "They told me it would be like this!" he exclaimed delightedly. "What fun!" Rosenblum gave as good as he got.

One of the principal contestants was always Gabriel Laderman. In those days, he tended to dress in denim overalls like a train engineer, his long hair sticking out beneath a crumpled cap that covered his balding head. His Cheshire Cat grin, marked by a gap between his front teeth, would hover in the air long after such meetings adjourned. Certainly, his eloquent arguments lingered in audiences' minds for years to come. But the Alliance wasn't just a battlefield for these figurative artists. There were also sweet interactions, as when Leland Bell would fill a carousel tray with slides of paintings that Laderman would then respond to off the cuff. After perhaps ten slides, Gabriel would say, "Ah, I see what you're up to," since the slide sequence would always have an agenda designed to trap or delight. The next week Gabriel might do the same for Leland. One could see the genuine affection and respect they felt for each other. And even when Laderman did lose control, as often as not he would be contrite just minutes later, sheepishly wondering if he had hurt anyone's feelings.

The Alliance was heady stuff, and perfect for a younger painter, because while Laderman spoke of a life well lived in art, that had nothing to do with having a career. It was as if the soul of the world hung in the balance, and we all had to take responsibility for what our work would mean. After all, our country was then embroiled in a catastrophic military debacle halfway around the world; the government was not to be trusted; and people had taken to the streets. Issues, even artistic ones, were all interrelated. One had to take a stand.

THE TEACHER

Something similar applied at Queens College, where Laderman taught from 1967 to 1996. Students tended to dread visits from the "Gang of Five," the group of painter/professors who prowled from studio to studio giving critiques, likely to spend as much energy dissecting each other as one's work. If Elias Friedensohn was on your committee, one could hear sotto voce warnings, "Eli's coming, better hide your art," and God help you if Laderman and Louie Finkelstein entered your studio together. Students tended to pledge allegiance to one or the other, or, more accurately, if you spent more time with Gabriel, Louie would avoid you like the plague. Like Mutt and Jeff, or a squabbling Don Quixote and Sancho Panza, the tall, skinny Finkelstein would put a hand over his heart on hearing what the shorter, rounder Laderman had to say, warning that this had to stop before he had another heart attack. Their joint critiques resembled the battle between Carnival and Lent, though they took turns alternately personifying Lenten rigor or carnivalesque outrageousness. We were in art boot camp, one filled with blustering, red-faced, merciless sergeants. The acoustics of the art building, a huge Quonset hut left over from World War II, let us hear shouts from ongoing critiques, as when Gabriel yelled at a grad student for being STUPID!!! Being a feisty New Yorker, the student yelled right back, ordering him to *Get the hell out of my studio NOW!*

Even the more subdued Robert Birmelin could be heard yelling the "S" word when a student provocatively said he only painted the way he did because his teachers at Kansas City Art Institute's undergrad program had told him to. And when Lennart Anderson came from Brooklyn College to give private crits, he announced he didn't like anything he saw, and even advised one kid to drop out for his own good. This was a sink-or-swim program, and I felt extremely lucky to be there.

I lived on West End Avenue across from the apartment where Laderman and his family have lived for decades. Four times a week I would catch a ride with Gabriel out to Queens College, the graduate program I had expressly chosen in order to shadow his every move. As his assistant, I saw him teach, and I went on to use some of his approaches in my subsequent teaching at the college level. Yet Queens undergrads seemed not to know what to make of the alternately grinning and shouting, kindly and

fearsome figure who stood before them, a New York version of Buddha/Kali. Laderman's generation grew up on the passions of the thirties, a world where comrades, inches away on the political spectrum, might be more reviled than polar opposites, and this intensity carried over to their art. On my rides out to Queens, I was more likely to hear quite specific objections to a recent show by one of his colleagues than a diatribe about someone at the other end of the spectrum, like Donald Judd or Andy Warhol. Over the years, Gabriel seems to have mellowed somewhat, and his current blog favors praise over blame.

I apprenticed myself informally to Gabriel in an effort to internalize his thought processes. Clearly he had his biases and considered the metaphorical implications of pictorial structure paramount, shying away from emotional content. After all, his generation was reacting against the often intentionally inarticulate emotionalism of their elders, the pursuit of the ineffable that too often worked as a dodge for teachers who had nothing much to offer. Laderman assumed students would bring their own stories to the work and that his job was to make them visually literate enough to find a voice for what they had to say.

In addressing issues of spatial organization, Laderman faced any number of misunderstandings shared by the whole culture, including the assumption that pictorial space automatically means the use of perspective. This speaks to the general lack of understanding of the vast array of choices developed over time and in widespread cultures for making pictorial worlds.

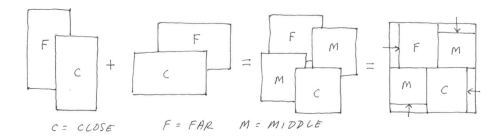

C = CLOSE   F = FAR   M = MIDDLE

Laderman taught one approach to pictorial architecture that I continue to find both very useful and liberating as a seed for other fruit. Gabriel's students were made to consider a spectrum from highly conceptualized drawing, as if from the mind's eye, to an approach as closely based on careful observation as possible. Like other artist/teachers seeking some continuity with recent tradition and connection to observed nature, he stressed the perceptual drawing of Cézanne, where one concentrates on and draws only the small visual incidents defined by plane changes or overlaps. The resulting meander through space carves a path into depth that has no preconceived goal or overriding organization. If perspective posits a box of space to be filled with obedient and discrete objects, Cézanne's approach lets space be created by the act of looking, where there are no objects per se, only visual footholds that allow us to climb up and into depth. If students work carefully in this snail's trail way, inevitably their initial and final marks will not correlate in any perspectival sense.

Whether we find the distortions in Cézanne's work exhilarating, disturbing, or some mixture of the two, the shifts, tilts, and splits before our eyes build a subtle pictorial analogy for the processes of perception. As one carves an arabesque into depth and back out again, these little plane changes and overlaps start to cohere as spatial locations sequentially identifiable as close, middle, far, middle, and back out to close. Since that which is lower tends to be read as closer, Laderman suggested students look for pictorial pressures that push down and there-fore forward on one or the other side of their sheet of paper. If a vertical is felt or found somewhere near the page's center, one could then literalize this shift by cutting the paper and moving the close half down, exaggerating the sensation of proximity. Taping the pieces together, one can then find a horizontal axis and cut and shift accordingly as in the above diagram.

Having gradually gone from small, local overlaps observed in the motif to four simplified overlapping spatial zones, students would then look for pressures near the periphery of the format that made for a crunching shift near the center, somewhat the way tectonic plates build and release tremendous pent up pressure. Laderman would show them works by Vermeer, Ingres, Courbet, and Cézanne that all share this underlying nonperspectival order.

The better students not only got some sense of surface shifts as communicating implied spatial pushes, but a sense that any number of other similarly subtle approaches to space can be found as well. For Gabriel never presented this as some arcane secret key to art, but as a vivid metaphor, somewhat the way the French theorist Roger de Piles described Rubens's work as often resembling a bunch of grapes, which curves toward us not just in the aggregate but as a collection of smaller, bulging centers of interest. Students need this kind of common-sense, sensate analogy in order to proceed, and that was where Gabriel always came through. Theory for its own sake was of no particular interest. Anything that would help students go forth and think for themselves was carefully cultivated. A significant number of people studied with Gabriel, and I would guess that not a single one of them ever forgot the experience.

THE PAINTER: EARLY WORK

But even if Laderman enjoyed the occasional fight at the Alliance, and if his social conscience led him to help educate succeeding generations, painters live to paint. He was part of the robust international postwar effort to find ways to reinform the figure, an effort overshadowed by the noisy success of abstract expressionism. Early on Laderman read Klee's *Pedagogical Sketchbook* and studied with Hans Hofmann and de Kooning in an effort to find pictorial structures that could contribute to a new, post-abstract figuration. His teachers were anything but doctrinaire and drew on a vast range of world art.

Ad Reinhardt pointed out how curving Arabic calligraphy played off against the often severe symmetry of Islamic architecture. He showed what Laderman recalls as "slides of the interiors of Hindu and Buddhist temples that were so dark it was almost impossible to make out the figures," which shed light on Reinhardt's black paintings.

Others gave hard-headed exercises in finding structures in the overlooked: "Alfred Russell had us not only drawing in the Natural History museum," writes Laderman, "but also highly touted the value of drawing parked cars, looking through the windows into the internal spaces, and those as seen in a second car through a first one." In his own work, Russell, a painter/teacher Laderman greatly admired, replaced Albertian perspective with non-Euclidean geometry as the locale for his haunted, invented, falling figures. As a teacher, Russell stressed immersing oneself in the nonobjective art idiom as a way to reinvigorate figuration, while avoiding the academic varieties of realism, or those that superficially borrow the look of abstraction. Russell could be wry: "The challenge of drawing and painting the figure is a formidable one, enough to have occupied the whole history of civilization; certainly it will be enough to occupy me as a painter." Or he could throw Nietzschean thunderbolts: "I believe one must be out of key with the times in order to see them at all: one must always be against the grain and never forget his contempt for the botched and bungled mob." He would regularly reduce graduate students to tears, for it was like studying with someone as mad and brilliant as Ezra Pound. Even Laderman found him intimidating.

A young painter's first European trip, where the figurative tradition hits you in the face like a frying pan, has to be equally intimidating. But a year in Italy on a Fulbright in 1962 seemed to clarify the issues for Laderman, who returned with the huge and powerful *View of Florence* (fig. 1). For me, it evokes Canaletto's *Stonemason's Yard* from 1727, roughly the same size, also an Italian cityscape, and also carefully using planar echoes of the picture plane as we step back into space. In particular, both paintings let spatial locations, separated by depth, kiss on the

Fig. 2. *Still Life #2, Homage to David,* 1969, p. 29

Fig. 1. *View of Florence,* 1962–63, p. 25

picture plane, letting large shadow diagonals assert shapes on the surface as well as carrying us into depth. In *View of Florence,* the little dance of triangular shapes in the lower right roofs is a wonderfully cubistic moment. But while Laderman dares to care about past art, this is not pastiche in any sense. He is announcing a new visual order as startling in its way as the work of Frank Stella or Donald Judd. This is a high level of pictorial intelligence brought to bear on the visible world, but it is also a manifesto of sorts, a glove thrown down to the New York art world. And it quickly finds American expression in the landscapes done in New Orleans and North Adams on his return.

The work from the sixties, such as *Still Life #2, Homage to David* (1969, fig. 2), looks cool, even austere. And how can we reconcile this austerity with his later work? Laderman feels it is all of a piece, and the more we look at the body of work, the more we can see it as all shaped by the same sensibility. The title of Laderman's painting cues us to remember Jacques-Louis David's *Death of Marat* (1793, fig. 3). We notice myriad shared traits: a clinical white light falls from the upper left, a large relatively unmodulated dark shape hovers above and behind a series of forms. These forms are subtly analogous in themselves.

For Marat's head, the jug to the far left; for his arm, the vertical white cylinder; and so on until the gelatin mold that projects out reminds us of Marat's box/writing desk. Interestingly, by this reading the egg in the still life, the only organic form we find, is analogous to the letter from Charlotte Corday that seals the revolutionary's fate. Is this all just cleverness, an in-joke? Consider when Laderman's painting was done: 1969, right after Martin Luther King Jr. and Robert Kennedy were shot and killed. All three leaders, Marat, King, and Kennedy, were assassinated in times of unpredictable change, of fervor, division, and rancor. These works by David and Laderman share an elegiac tone, a sense that tragedy is best seen with realistic clarity. They have an almost fatalistically geometric inevitability, as if we are all locked in to a big, cosmic picture. Again and again for Laderman, still-life objects and configurations are stand-ins for much larger forces.

Fig. 3. Jacques-Louis David, French (1748–1825), *Death of Marat,* 1793, oil on canvas, 165 x 128 cm., Musee d'Art Ancien, Musees Royaux des Beaux-Arts, Brussels, Belgium, ©Scala/Art Resource, N.Y.

Fig. 4. *View of North Adams*, 1968, p. 27

Something similarly metaphysical haunts the *View of North Adams* (1968, fig. 4) from about the same time, a work that shares some of the ghost-town quality of Hopper's iconic *Early Sunday Morning*. While Hopper and Laderman locate themselves to face a planar wall of buildings, the latter places himself higher and farther away, making the landscape resemble a self-contained still life. As in the *View of Florence,* different spatial locations both open up and pinch to the surface in the *View of North Adams*: the left edge of the aqua-blue building lines up with edges and plane changes farther back, so the intervening street is both credibly navigable and blocked by surface pattern. This turquoise foreground rectangle seems to hover up to the picture plane, partly because of its color weight (something Laderman learned from Hoffman), partly because its cast shadow helps it mimic a bas-relief. I find this geometry reassuring, as if a reliable order can be found in, or made of, the world.

These early paintings, bathed in their cool white light, show a profound interest in combining the observed with some underlying order. Laderman was always interested in perception's tug of war with conception and had the odd gift of a Cézanne-like hand that made subtle distortions flow naturally into his constructed spaces. If nature and nurture filter our perception, then some will classicize or idealize what they see, while others resist such cleaning up, finding an expressionism based on both making and finding.

Consider the huge jug in Laderman's *Still Life with Large Ceramic Jug* (1972, fig. 5). On the left it sags as if pregnant, almost touching the table leg, while on the right it lifts like a hot-air balloon, nudging our eye up along the format's right edge. This may be the product of the incremental working method he taught in class, and such distortions certainly show up in Chardin and Cézanne, painters resisting the conceptualized, cleaned-up symmetry of those who want to get it "right." Yet the table suggests something even odder. If the jug seems stretched back and to the right, the table appears to pull us up and into depth on the left. One can argue that the world seems to expand out and away from us as credibly or sensibly as it contracts to a vanishing point. Laderman's still life encourages such a reading, for his table expands rather than shrinking as it recedes to the left. (Not to mention the legs, which splay as they go down.) And then the relentlessly white rectangularity of the side of the table seems to pull us back out to the surface at the same time it promises recession.

Fig. 5. *Still Life with Large Ceramic Jug*, 1972, p. 31

Perhaps this tension helps explain some of our unease as we stand before this work. People quickly notice the limited palette, which works as warm and cool, based on an overall pink tonality. The analytic cubists similarly avoided saturated color as a part of their controlled formal experimentation. Juan Gris would be happy with these large unmodulated shapes, alternately tipping us in and out of space and hugging the surface. For just as we start to accept the harsh realism of this still life with jug, Laderman undercuts the promise of rationality with a teasing sense of unease. Objectivity is first posited, then withdrawn. The more we assume we know, the less we really do. Finally, for this viewer, there is something anthropomorphic about all of these interactions, as if a large, solid man looks up at a world of lesser beings who try to lord it over him, but still stands free of their shadow. One is tempted to consider the jug a kindred spirit with Brunelleschi's dome in the *View of Florence,* or to see them both as symbolic self-portraits.

Similar thinking applies in *Portrait of Johanna* (1972, fig. 6). Shifts in the box, the wall, and the chair's architecture result from Laderman's rigorously perceptual approach and are accepted as pictorial pressures, reminding us of the shifting squares diagram (see page 8). Using its logic, we find an implied vertical running down through her right hand. Since the right half of the space is generally closer, look for pressure up and back on the left, here suggested by the harsh shadow line at Johanna's feet. This push is answered by implied pressure down on her head, relative to the top edge of the painting. Now cut a horizontal through her lap, look for completion of the circuit in a vertical in the upper left (the shadow line or the wall division), pushing us to the right.

Fig. 6. *Portrait of Johanna*, 1972, p. 32

This is answered by the push we get to the left in the form of the vertical rear chair leg. Literalize these quadrants as chair—close, Johanna's leg—middle, wall—far, torso—middle, back to where we began. In fact, her slumping posture and raised leg cooperate nicely in this overall shift, as her pose becomes a sort of whirling cross, all rotating around the pivotal hand in her lap. We can also see the overall organization as bulging toward us and curving away on the periphery and find any number of subtle pictorial surprises here. As viewers we're not always asked to delineate, or even to consciously register, pictorial mechanics, any more than we necessarily follow the sonata form's structural intricacies as we listen to Bach. However, at times, as in the *Large Malaysian Still Life* (1976, fig. 7), where the shifting squares become quite clear, structure itself is advertised for poetic reasons and with cosmological allusions.

We come back to the malaise mentioned earlier, this queasy undertone. Johanna is not idealized or particularly attractive, and she sits alone on a harshly lit stage like a character from a Beckett play. With no social or domestic context, no attributes to clarify her role or identity, she is emotionally naked, confronted by a viewer/artist who projects onto her and even shares her fatalistic wait. Outlined in the kind of brittle light that makes Morandi's early still lifes into metaphysical poems, she is locked into her own shadow, her own stark world, as a volumetric silhouette. Like Joe Friday in the old TV show, *Dragnet*, we think we're getting "just the facts ma'am, nothing but the facts," a no-

Fig. 7. *Large Malaysian Still Life*, 1976, p. 33

nonsense American literalism. But why do we feel so uneasy? Especially in this early work we feel a kind of one-two punch, suckered in by objectivity until the subjectivity at the core of experience begins to haunt us.

THE PAINTER: LATER WORK

In 1975, Laderman accompanied his anthropologist wife, Carol, to Malaysia, where she was doing work on childbirth and studying an indigenous pre-Islamic system of hot and cool humors in shamanistic medicine. In Malaysia a shaman asked Laderman what painting was for. "To change people," said Gabriel. "Does it work?" asked the shaman. Apparently getting away from the New York art world was in itself life-changing for Laderman. True, taking the Lincoln Tunnel to New Jersey takes you to a world that could not possibly care less about the arcana of the art scene in Manhattan or Brooklyn. But when a wise man from a totally unfamiliar culture asks about the activity you've been immersed in all your life, wanting to know what it's for, and whether it works, you take the question seriously.

View of Kuala Lumpur with Birds (1982, fig. 8), is as lighthearted as its subject. Gabriel identifies with these birds, perhaps feeling freed from the occasionally smug provincialism of New York. They seem like Jackson Pollocks done after nature, describing or implying loopy trajectories, a touching tribute to free spirits caught on the fly. Coming back from Malaysia, Laderman spoke of things he might have disdained in the past, such as alpha

waves and meditation. An experiment had impressed him, one that hooked up artists to monitors. Apparently, when deeply engaged in painting, their brain waves were indistinguishable from those of people meditating. The Ladermans' son, Michael, had suffered from what they were told was an incurable malady, but had been verifiably helped by a Malaysian faith healer, and Carol had benefited from going into a trance at the hands of a shaman practicing a type of precognitive therapy. It appeared that Laderman's two sides, the cool, deeply rational man and the expressionist hot head, could be reconciled as if by magic. And that magic could be given form through art. Art isn't therapy for the artist, but it helps make sense of an errant and elusive world. After Malaysia, Laderman's work became more and more thoughtfully wild or wildly thoughtful.

Fig. 8. *View of Kuala Lumpur with Birds*, 1982, p. 35

Another wry comment on his own nature might be found in *Still Life with Order and Chaos* (1983–84, fig. 9, location unknown). Any visitor to Laderman's apartment or studio would know the chaos part came easily, and the order is clear just in the act of painting. Chaos theory tries to find the point at which order, like a quiet thread of cigarette smoke, devolves into randomness, as when the smoke begins to curl into unpredictable swirls. Physicist David Bohm's idea of implicate order, one that finds flow as preexisting the "things" that form and dissolve into this flow, might also be applied to the human detritus in the neglected corners of our lives. We could again read this still life as a surrogate self-portrait, and in fact Gabriel's leg shows up in the mirror to the far left, draped in the checkered batik material he tended to favor after living in Malaysia. Order and chaos, cool and hot, life and death; Emerson and Whitman famously asked us to take such seeming contradictions and to grow because of them, to encompass multitudes.

Fig. 9. *Still Life with Order and Chaos,* 1983–84, p. 39

At this time, Laderman began a whole series of powerful paintings based on mystery novels. Working on narratives of crime was not a self-consciously canny strategy: Gabriel and Carol had personally witnessed a murder in a convenience store on the Upper West Side. Violence, like class or race, is inherent in our history, whether we like it or not. At first, as in 1984's three-part *Murder and Its Consequences* (fig. 10), Laderman's white light of careful observation falls on a clinically clear sequence. There are foreshortenings that place us physically in the space and emotionally in the mind of the criminal. Goya's *Disasters of War*, with their captions, "I saw this" or "This happens," share Laderman's stark realism, the sense of being implicated in human cruelty. But with *The House of Death*

and Life (1984–85, fig. 11), a process implicit from the beginning starts to manifest itself more and more emphatically.

Being a collector, Gabriel bought a large antique doll house, thinking it would serve as the proscenium stage for a complex narrative, and put it in one of the rabbit-warren rooms of his West End Avenue apartment. There it stayed for years, languishing amidst the chaotic clutter, until he read the work of Georges Simenon, the French detective writer, at which point the neglected doll house came into its own. Most of us are probably unfamiliar with Simenon's *Maigret and the Spinster*, and as a result, we become the detective as we face this multipanel painting, puzzling out just what is going on. A murder appears to be taking place in the upper left room, and two witnesses apparently hear noises above them. A prone man dreams or hallucinates a woman's naked torso, while under him two women share a kitchen. There's enough symmetry, polarization, and doubling here to make the anthropologist Lévi-Strauss feel right at home. A dysfunctional home. And like the anthropologist, we seek some structuralist logic, coming up with readings the way we do when we "read" the gridlike panels of Duccio's *Maesta* or a Torres-García painting.

Pairs and dichotomies abound. Two women above one sitting man are diagonally across from two women below one prone man. The first female pair is intimate in the act of strangulation, the latter alienated and avoiding contact. The lower left man is alert, sensing trouble in the present, the upper right man

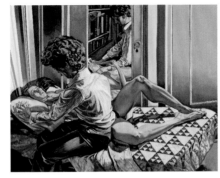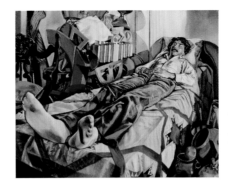

Fig. 10. *Murder and Its Consequences*, 1984, p. 36–38

is presumably asleep, perhaps dreaming of past or future love. Upstairs the light is dim, the shadows soft, at least in contrast to the klieg light penumbras below, as if light itself is a major clue. We sense conscious clarity versus murky desire. Death to the upper left, love to the upper right. Shards of light are clues as informative as all the chairs, some relentlessly vertical, some knocked about at random. Then there are the poles of hot and cool, epitomized by the kitchen's ironically hot icebox and cool stove, which finds some echo in the women themselves. If the (stove) woman in the nightgown is overall cool, she emerges into the hall as our rational detective-proxy, out to solve the doll-house crime. More clues emerge gradually. Why is our view so close to floor level in one room, while the neighboring floor tilts up dramatically to meet our eye? What of the scale changes from figure to figure and the huge heads some of them have? The upper hallway becomes an emblem for the whole quiet mystery, resonating like an early de Chirico. The murder itself is so quiet we begin to strain our ears the way the witnesses do.

The polarities in *The House of Death and Life* might remind us of the world-view described by Gabriel's wife, Carol, in her books on the humoral system of the Malay shaman. Poles of "cool" and "hot" govern a complex cosmological, social, and medical system intriguing both on its literal and metaphoric levels. Echoes might be found in Western dichotomies: those of Nietzsche (Apollonian and Dionysian), Freud, Lévi-Strauss, or Mondrian (the theosophical implications of horizontal and vertical). In the Malay system, "cold" is healthy and life giving, but is balanced by "hot," which, while associated with excrement, misfortune, and death, is necessary for the whole. *Angin*, the term for the varieties of wind that blow "hot" or "cold," determines all forms of health, from the individual to the cosmic.

This pre-Islamic Malay system has long diagnosed an ill wind of increasing heat and unhealthiness (and this, even before global warming). The *minduk* is the master of the inner winds, the interpreter of the shaman's trances, and here Carol Laderman's studies could apply to her husband's way of seeing. Buddhists call the human body the "burning house." Laderman's painting suggests a bicameral mind, a conflicted body, a house divided against itself. Then again, it might evoke the *minduk's* ability to reconcile opposites. In any case, a shift becomes apparent in Laderman's work with this painting. From the start he is a rational man filled with passionate intensity. Now cool edges over into hot as some personal sluice is opened.

Fig. 11. *The House of Death and Life*, 1984–85, p. 41

Family Romance I (1988–89, fig. 12) is clearly by the same man who painted *Portrait of Johanna*, for the simplifications, distortions, and animated shadows remain, if in a heightened state. The space in both works shears away diagonally on either

15

side of a central entry. Narrative has entered the later picture, making the artist a kind of director, staging a play in which the actors are absorbed in their drama rather than addressing the viewer/painter. I read this as a cast of two, with the nude being a homuncular version of the clothed woman, perhaps even a fantasy in one or both characters' minds. If we cover this nude, the rest of the space may still be strange, but it becomes easily legible, so she seems purposely disjunctive both spatially and psychologically. There is a parallel to the interaction of man and nude in the shadow play farther back, where she grows from his hirsute head to reach toward his antishadow with a little wolf-like hand. Both her yellow square of light, which fails to follow the plane change marked out by the floor molding, and the black aura that surrounds her, take the nude into another order of being, whether it be dream, memory, or wish fulfillment.

Fig. 12. *Family Romance I*, 1988–89, p. 43

Given the painting's title, we're cued to think of Freud's term for the process of individuation within the family. The good doctor tells us that the child feels a sexual attraction for the parent of the opposite gender, so one might read this as the now grown male child craving the attentions of his mother or perhaps the woman recalling her craving for her father. Of course, there may be other readings. Since the clothed man and woman seem to look at each other, this nude may be something coming between them and is not necessarily what he opens his arms to receive. The availability of multiple readings contributes to the dream-like aspect of the whole, making the performance leave the stage and enter the subconscious. Never noticeably fond of the surrealists, Laderman does seem to borrow their use of credible, if disjunctive objectivity to remind us how dreams feel. And if the shadow play to the left owes something to surrealism, then late Braque or early Morandi comes to mind as holding our feet to the metaphysical fire. The wild and wonderful table below the somehow solid yet negative shadow of the man's head may hold the whole painting in microcosm. We may work to decipher or disentangle the table legs and their spidery shadows or let their complexity capture us the way the narrative's questions do.

This Happens (1996–97, fig. 13) also might make us wonder who is actually here, who is doing the perceiving. What or who casts the shadows, which dance on the wall like the mountains in a Chinese brush painting? The big man may be our surrogate, so that as he loses consciousness the women shrink into a false distance, a psychological inaccessibility. While these women seem compassionate, Laderman's title evokes the terse summaries below each image of Goya's *Disasters of War*, the series of etchings about folly, cruelty, and death. Gabriel has suffered from a rare form of leukemia for some time now, and though he has managed to keep it at bay, he must be more haunted by death than those of us still convinced we have time to burn. We recall the shaman's question when we read Annie Dillard: "Write as if you were dying. At the same time, assume you write for an audience consisting solely of terminal patients. That is, after all, the case. What would you begin writing if you knew you would die soon? What could you say to a dying person that would not enrage by its triviality?"

THE WRITER

In articles published from 1966 on and more recently in his blog, Laderman has put significant effort into writing about the problems faced by serious artists. Several generations of painters interested in what Laderman calls unconventional realism, or more recently, post-abstract figuration, have looked to him as a mentor, a somewhat cantankerous father figure. "Being and Becoming" (*Art Journal*, Winter 1966) describes what Laderman considered two ultimately misleading theoretical options at the time. "Being" describes an approach which detaches art from its context in history and in the experiential world and makes it seem impersonally pure, as if quality can somehow be abstracted or detached from individual works of art. "Becoming" makes the artist a genius who rejects his time and place, pulling spectacular rabbits out of a self-created hat. But whether reduced to a cipher or elevated to some otherworldly height, the artist is removed from his "daily, plodding practice." Both viewpoints misunder-

stand tradition, treating it either as a "weight of formulas to be followed impersonally toward art" or as "outworn practices to be discarded or broken through." But if "being" can be traced to Parmenides, and "becoming" to Heraclitus, Laderman proposes a third, atomic model out of Democritus. Such a model sees each painting as an individual "atom," important in itself, with an artist's life work as a molecule within the super molecules of the body of world art. "Tradition, no longer oppressive, becomes breathable atmosphere. The artist picks and chooses among the 'atoms' of history. An evolution is now possible in which backward glance, individual idiosyncrasy, and representation of nature form one process."

Fig. 13. *This Happens*, 1996–97, p. 46

Laderman concludes, "Consciousness of the action of tradition is a necessity if the artist does not wish to remain tossed by the winds of change or trapped in the stasis of absolute direction and prohibition." This latter trap reminds one of the prescriptive power enjoyed at the time by Clement Greenberg. As Laderman points out, theories of "being" and "becoming" come to share an ahistorical rootlessness that deprives the artist of genuine volition. And history is at the root of Laderman's project—a profound conception of continuity that also allows for innovation.

His interest in and knowledge of world art is clear in an article on Cézanne also from 1966. Clearly, one can sense his identification with artists rebelling against the art world of their own day:

> Ni Tsan and Huang Kung-wang were two of the five revolutionaries of Yüan painting. They revolted against traditional Sung landscape painting, by then over-conventionalized, codified landscape composition painting in the studio without reference to nature. . . . Ni Tsan and his friends rejected, in proto-bohemian revolt, the whole official social trappings of art, became vagabonds and painted directly from nature. Their work has little orthodox meditational value; there is no road, there are no houses for meditation. On the other hand, it is possible to move from point to point, from stroke to stroke, from land form to land form, experiencing a spatiality reminiscent of the late Cézanne oils and watercolors. Their stroke, too, tends to become unvaried and concentrates on spatial flow rather than on object representation. The eye flows over the forms into deep recession with an effect of spatial realism never achieved before or afterwards in Chinese painting. . . . The similarity of their work and Cézanne's is the result of similarity of process and similarity of discoveries in the face of nature.

Laderman sees us caught in a quagmire of denatured conventionality analogous to that faced by other artists in history such as the Yüan brush painters, Giotto, the Carracci, Caravaggio, or by Cézanne himself. Like Antaeus, who regained his strength every time he touched the ground, these painters revivified art by returning to nature while informed by deep familiarity with their tradition. We tend to underrate the sophistication of artists of the past; even Clement Greenberg seemed to think that "old style" painting's sole aim was to perfect illusion as if slouching toward protophotography. Laderman had students read John White's brilliant *The Birth and Rebirth of Pictorial Space*, which made it very clear that early Renaissance artists were highly conscious of the surface and of preventing runaway recession into depth.

Such awareness runs all through our tradition and is hardly a twentieth-century invention. As a student in the early 1970s, I remember reading Gabriel's analysis of Corot's *The Mantes Bridge* in a piece called "The Outer Light" (*Art News Annual*, November 1969). There he draws attention to the curving trunks of foreground trees that assert the picture plane but also link up to more distant forms such as the arches of the bridge, making an elastic conversation between surface and depth. The red color note of the distant man in the boat pulls to the surface through its saturation and scale while the greatest tonal contrast is reserved for the ostensibly most distant zone, the houses in the upper left.

Laderman spoke of the nuts and bolts options in picture making as well as their underlying metaphoric or poetic implications. He presciently pointed out in 1970 ("Notes from the Underground") that the extremely long learning curve involved in this process of studio self-education did not jibe well with academic programs: "Just as the tendency in colleges is to teach that part of art which can most easily be expressed verbally and to value it most highly, the tendency of critics will be to value that art most highly which gives their words the most play." His was a very hands-on, careful exercise in vision, as we can see in "The Outer Light":

> Even the most technically conservative landscape painters were affected by the process of painting and studying from nature. Thomas Cole, in his early studies . . . decided emphatically that the outline of the forms should be arrived at only through a slow development of the interior, this in total disregard of Ingres's dictum that "line is the probity of art." The palette knife of Courbet, which he used to develop the volumes and spaces implicit in the shapes before them, became itself in many of his paintings a normative mark which defined small planes traveling through space and united the painting into an object of unified texture.

❧

The French Academy was founded in 1648 partly to elevate painting from a craft to a liberal art, so there is a history to denigrating studio practice in favor of philosophizing. By shoehorning the visual arts into Aristotle's *Poetics*, the academy tended to make painting literary and ideational. But Laderman reminds us how the beast is actually born, as here from the same article:

> Cézanne . . . did not use . . . hues only to arrive at chromatic equivalents of the lights, middle tones and darks which explain form, but instead for independent planar investigations of the forms in space presented to him by his motif. He used little planes of color traveling over forms and spaces in independent paths to describe the volumes and spaces observed. The independence from one another of their pictorial paths led to distortions of the outlines of forms. These were constantly reworked by the same procedure in a search for simplicity and monumentality. This procedure was responsible for the new plasticity, new not only to Cézanne, but, in this form, to the history of art.

❧

If you're trying to paint, this is the kind of help you need. Laderman's atomic model is also highly consoling. In "The Future of Landscape Painting" (*Artforum*, November 1968), he wrote: "Generations of pictorial solutions are available to us; . . . the representational painter . . . should recognize that there are no viable rules and boundaries to his activity and proclaim his freedom by discovering and inventing the ones he needs to make a viable poetic statement." He ended with an extended quote from Kuo Hsi, an eleventh-century Sung painter who describes a beautiful landscape as seen by a lover of forest and stream, which concludes: "Does not such a scene satisfy his mind and captivate his heart? That is why the world values the true significance of the painting of mountains. If this is not recognized, and the landscapes are roughly and carelessly approached, then is it not like spoiling a magnificent view and polluting the pure wind?"

One thinks of the current argument as to whether beauty is somehow misleading, a dishonest distraction from the cruelty around us. A man writing almost a millennium ago is warning us that art is our self-portrait as a species, and that we can pollute our art as easily as we pollute our world. In a letter further clarifying his "Notes from the Underground" (*Artforum*, September 1970), Laderman wrote:

> Rather than proselytizing for figuration exclusively I try to proselytize for an art of feeling, sensibility, and knowledge, whether figurative or abstract. . . . It is surely untenable for a contemporary artist or critic to think of art history in linear terms as a one- or two-way street. The linearity we prize is a useful construct of the art historians, but all the objects remain to be reexperienced and reinterpreted by those artists who do not fear history and do not need the crutch of a narrow contemporary self-congratulating elite to bolster their egos.

The article makes it clear that innovation (which incorporates feeling, sensibility, and knowledge) is essential:

> Virgil Thompson, writing some years ago in *Encounter*, said that if we divide the twentieth century into fifteen-year intervals, the amount of innovation within these decreases as they approach the present. This can be seen even more acutely in the art of the last ten years. Thompson continues to say that in the future, instead of quality following the new, the new will have to follow quality. I would go further and say that the new, which is the elite art of today, will have to develop more slowly if it is to be truly new. Artists must be given time to develop their eccentricities, which can no longer be limited by the standards of twentieth-century *avant-gardes*.

One senses his catholic taste, good faith, and essential optimism as the article continues:

> Young figurative artists are reading and using D'Arcy Thompson's *On Growth and Form*, the books of Matila Ghika and Jay Hambidge on proportion and geometry, restudying Albertian and other perspective systems and deriving inspiration from crystallography, geology, solid geometry, non-Euclidean geometry, and topology. The conceptual art which results from this kind of study is liable to lead some young artists toward abstraction, in this case an abstraction of intellect which will require an esoteric knowledge on the part of the beholder as well as the maker; in other words a true elite art.

In 1970, the war in Vietnam was at its height, and Laderman in this article also addressed art as an agent of change, arguing that Cézanne may emerge as more influential than Karl Marx: "The experience of a Cézanne painting, fragmenting, reforming, finally monumentalizing the forms and spaces in nature, had an insidious effect on the minds of those who experienced it." Such subtly vast influence can still be looked for from art:

> The artist who, like Giorgione, produces a poetic metaphor in structure, form, and subject matter, could once again become the inspiration of the poet and the intellectual. Such an artist, no matter how high his ivory tower, would not necessarily be apolitical in his effect. The artist, who through his imagination creates forms which change the vision of others, is potentially capable of changing the world more radically and more surely than the most successful and radical political philosopher.

This is a man highly ambitious not just for himself as an isolated ego but for the art he loves and sees as an inherently moral force. Gabriel Laderman has consistently advocated thoughtfulness over excitement, poetic meaning over novelty, and has been telling us, in his urgent, angry, and loving way, that we can and must do better.

A friend, the poet Charles Wright, heard my frustrated complaint that whatever it is I sought in my work always seemed to elude me. "Well, when you stop feeling like that, you can stop altogether," he wisely pointed out. Artists could consider Sisyphus their patron saint, for I've never met one entirely free

21

from severe crises of confidence, retrospective panics about whether they have done their best. And my brother, a scientist, asked when I knew when a painting was done, for unlike his experiments, nothing could verify some final success, some incontrovertible proof. So how are we to evaluate Laderman's success, given his stated goals? His track record as a teacher is established, his writings are equally clear, and his own work has become a wonderfully discrete molecule in the atomic model he himself outlined in 1966. It has a coherent form in itself, with the subtle complexities of a rich multivalent carbon compound whose internal symmetries continue to baffle and move us. Should some future exhibition, equivalent to Rosenblum's The Age of Revolution, set out to give a more comprehensive view of late-twentieth-century art, Laderman will certainly be there, front and center in the section on the new post-abstract figuration. This selective retrospective will help set the record straight about the power and poetry of this body of work, this life spent well in art. Like Democritus's atom, Laderman's work stands available and inviolable.

Lincoln Perry
University of Virginia

PAINTINGS

1. *View of Florence*, 1962–63, oil on canvas, 49 ¾ x 70 inches, Collection of the artist

2. *View of St. Joseph's Cathedral, Baton Rouge*, 1967, oil on canvas, 40 x 50 inches, Collection of the Catholic Diocese of Baton Rouge

3. *View of North Adams*, 1968, oil on canvas, 40 x 50 inches, Collection of Malcolm Holzman

4. *Still Life*, 1969, oil on canvas, 36 x 45 inches, Collection of the artist

5. *Still Life #2, Homage to David*, 1969, oil on canvas, 40 x 50 inches, Collection of Dr. and Mrs. Edmund Pillsbury

6. *Still Life #5*, 1970, oil on canvas, 40 x 50 inches, Collection of the artist

7. *Still Life with Large Ceramic Jug*, 1972, oil on canvas, 40 x 40 inches, Innes Collection

8. *Portrait of Johanna*, 1972, oil on canvas, 40 x 40 inches, Collection of the artist

9. *Large Malaysian Still Life*, 1976, oil on canvas, 44 x 56 inches, The Spurzem Family Collection

10. *View of Kuala Lumpur IV*, 1972, oil on canvas, 45 x 64 inches, The Spurzem Family Collection

11. *View of Kuala Lumpur with Birds*, 1982, oil on canvas, 27 ½ x 36 inches, Innes Collection

12a. *Murder and Its Consequences*, 1984, oil on canvas, 1 of 3 panels: 45 x 36 inches, Collection of the artist

12b. *Murder and Its Consequences*, 1984, oil on canvas, 2 of 3 panels: 36 x 45 inches, Collection of the artist

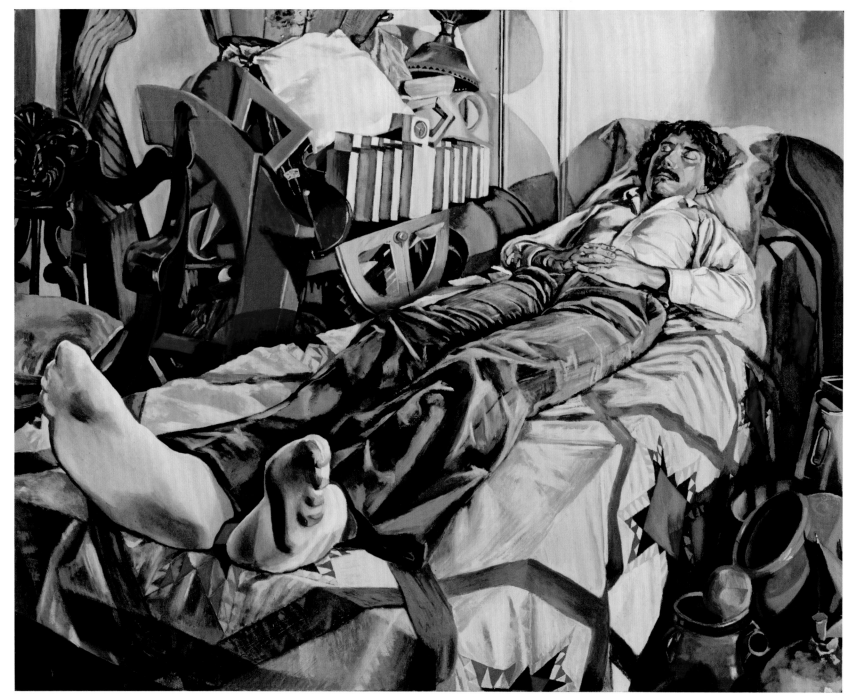

12c. *Murder and Its Consequences*, 1984, oil on canvas, 3 of 3 panels: 36 x 45 inches, Collection of the artist

13. *Still Life with Order and Chaos*, 1983–84, oil on canvas, 28 x 36 inches (location unknown)

14. *Study for House of Death and Life*, 1985, oil on canvas, 45 x 36 inches, Collection of the artist

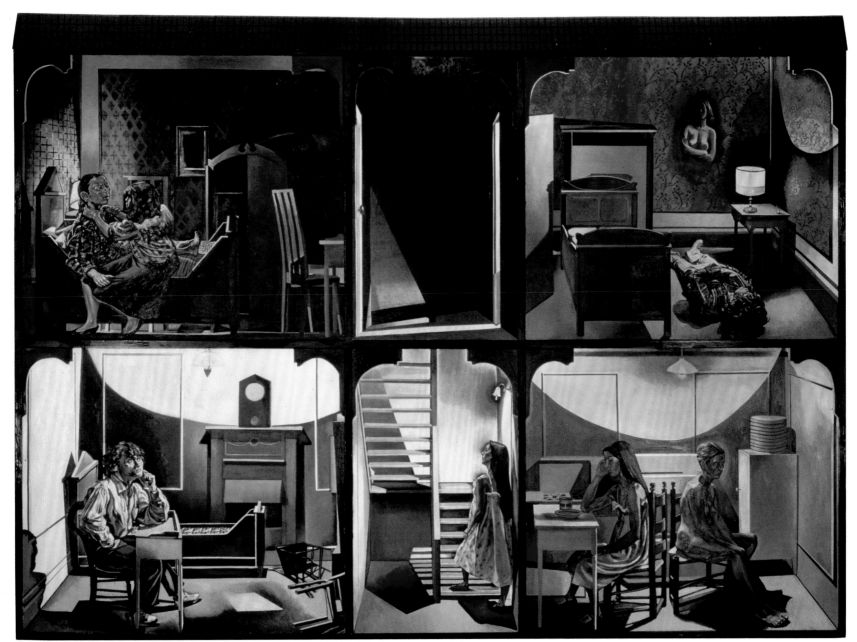

15. *The House of Death and Life*, 1984–85, oil on canvas, 93 x 135 inches, Collection of the artist

16. *The Dream*, 1988, oil on canvas, 72 x 90 inches, Collection of the artist

17. *Family Romance I*, 1988–89, oil on canvas, 72 x 108 inches, Collection of the artist

18. *Nymph and Satyr II*, 1990, oil on canvas, 60 x 72 inches, Collection of the artist

19. *The Dance of Death*, 1995–96, oil on canvas, 72 x 90 inches, Collection of the artist

20. *This Happens*, 1996–97, oil on canvas, 72 x 72 inches, Collection of the artist

EXHIBITION CHECKLIST

Dimensions are in inches, height preceding width. Unless otherwise noted, works are in the collection of the artist.

1. *View of Florence*, 1962–63
   oil on canvas, 49 ¾ x 70

2. *View of St. Joseph's Cathedral,*
   Baton Rouge, 1967
   oil on canvas, 40 x 50
   Collection of the Catholic Diocese
   of Baton Rouge

3. *View of North Adams*, 1968
   oil on canvas, 40 x 50
   Collection of Malcolm Holzman

4. *Still Life*, 1969
   oil on canvas, 36 x 45

5. *Still Life #2, Homage to David*, 1969
   oil on canvas, 40 x 50
   Collection of Dr. and Mrs. Edmund
   Pillsbury

6. *Still Life #5*, 1970
   oil on canvas, 40 x 50

7. *Still Life with Large Ceramic Jug*, 1972
   oil on canvas, 40 x 40
   Innes Collection

8. *Portrait of Johanna*, 1972
   oil on canvas, 40 x 40

9. *Large Malaysian Still Life*, 1976
   oil on canvas, 44 x 56
   The Spurzem Family Collection

10. *View of Kuala Lumpur IV*, 1972
    oil on canvas, 45 x 64
    The Spurzem Family Collection

11. *View of Kuala Lumpur with Birds*, 1982
    oil on canvas, 27 ½ x 36
    Innes Collection

12. *Murder and Its Consequences*, 1984
    oil on canvas, 3 panels: 45 x 36, 36 x 45,
    36 x 45

13. *Still Life with Order and Chaos*, 1983–84
    oil on canvas, 28 x 36
    (location unknown)

14. *Study for House of Death and Life*, 1985
    oil on canvas, 45 x 36

15. *The House of Death and Life*, 1984–85
    oil on canvas, 93 x 135

16. *The Dream*, 1988
    oil on canvas, 72 x 90

17. *Family Romance I*, 1988–89
    oil on canvas, 72 x 108

18. *Nymph and Satyr II*, 1990
    oil on canvas, 60 x 72

19. *The Dance of Death*, 1995–96
    oil on canvas, 72 x 90

20. *This Happens*, 1996–97
    oil on canvas, 72 x 72

GABRIEL LADERMAN: RÉSUMÉ AND BIBLIOGRAPHY

Born Brooklyn, N.Y., 1929

EDUCATION

Cornell University, M.F.A., 1957

Brooklyn College, B.A., 1952

Studied in the studio of Willem de Kooning, 1949–50

Hans Hofmann School, summer 1949

Atelier 17, with S.W. Hayter, 1949, 1952

HONORS, AWARDS, COMMISSIONS

1995	National Academy of Design, Altman Prize
1993	National Academy of Design, Thomas R. Proctor Prize
1990	Ingram-Merrill Award
1989	Rockefeller Foundation, Resident Artist at Bellagio
1988	Queens College Presidential Fellowship
	John Simon Guggenheim Memorial Fellowship
	CUNY Research Foundation
1987	National Endowment for the Arts Senior Fellowship
1986	CUNY Research Award
1983	Ingram-Merrill Award
1982	National Endowment for the Arts Senior Fellowship
	CUNY Research Award
1975	Department of the Interior, Bicentennial Landscape Commission
	Ingram-Merrill Award
1973	CUNY Research Award
1962	Fulbright Award to Italy
1960	Yaddo Fellowship
1959	Yaddo Fellowship
	Louis Comfort Tiffany Award

TEACHING

American University, 1995–96, Visiting Distinguished Professor

Queens College, Professor, 1967–1996; Chairman, Art Department, 1979–82

Godwin-Ternbach Museum, Founding Director, 1980–82

American University Distinguished Visiting Faculty, 1967–68

Yale University, Visiting Professor, Graduate School, 1989, 1983, 1982, 1981, 1968–69.

Queens College Summer Landscape Program at Caumsett State Park, Founding Director 1980–81

Yale-Norfolk School, Instructor of Painting, 1974

Louisiana State University, Artist in Residence, 1966–67

Tanglewood Institute, Master Class in Painting, 1973

Skowhegan School of Painting and Sculpture, Senior Faculty, 1970, 1971

Pratt Institute, Assistant Professor, 1959–68
SUNY-New Paltz, Assistant Professor, 1957–59

SELECTED SOLO EXHIBITIONS

1997 Tatistcheff & Co., New York, N.Y.

1994 Tatistcheff & Co., New York, N.Y.

1991 Contemporary Realist Gallery, San Francisco, Calif.

1990 Robert Schoelkopf Gallery, New York, N.Y.

1987 Jessica Darraby Gallery, Los Angeles, Calif.
Contemporary Realist Gallery, San Francisco, Calif.

1986 Robert Schoelkopf Gallery, New York, N.Y.

1983 Mead Art Museum, Amherst College, Amherst, Mass.

1982 Cornell University, Ithaca, N.Y.
National Museum of Malaysia, Kuala Lumpur

1978 Institute of International Education, United Nations, New York, N.Y.

1977 Dart Gallery, Chicago, Ill.
Robert Schoelkopf Gallery, New York, N.Y.

1975 Sunne Savage Gallery, Boston, Mass.

1974 Robert Schoelkopf Gallery, New York, N.Y.

1972 Robert Schoelkopf Gallery, New York, N.Y.
Tyler School of Art, Temple University, Elkins Park, Pa.
Harwood Gallery, Springfield, Mo.

1970 Hobart College, Geneva, N.Y.

1969 Robert Schoelkopf Gallery, New York, N.Y.

1966 Louisiana State University, Baton Rouge, La.

1964 Robert Schoelkopf Gallery, New York, N.Y.

SELECTED GROUP EXHIBITIONS

2005 Poetic Dimensions in the Modern Still Life (Zeuxis exhibition), traveled to Hofstra Museum, Hempstead, N.Y.; Kouros Gallery, New York, N.Y.; DuPont Gallery, Washington and Lee University, Lexington, Va.

2004 Tabletop Arenas (Zeuxis exhibition), traveled to Colby College Museum of Art, Waterville, Maine; Lori Bookstein Fine Art, New York, N.Y.; The Art Gallery, University of New Hampshire, Durham, N.H.; Cantor Fitzgerald Gallery, Haverford College, Haverford, Pa.; Ohr-O'Keefe Museum of Art, Biloxi, Miss.

2000 The Human Presence (Zeuxis exhibition), traveled to University Gallery, University of Wisconsin at La Crosse, Wis.; Peninsula Fine Arts Center, Newport News, Va.; Courtyard Gallery, Washington Studio School, Washington, D.C.; Erector Square Gallery, New Haven, Conn.; The Painting Center, New York, N.Y.

2000 American Academy of Arts and Letters, New York, N.Y.

1998 Summer 1998 Group Exhibition, Tatistcheff & Co., New York, N.Y.

1997   Anniversary Exhibition, Hackett-Freedman Gallery,
        San Francisco, Calif.

1994   Summer Gallery Group Exhibition, Tatistcheff & Co.,
        New York, N.Y.

1992   New American Figure Painting, Contemporary Realist
        Gallery, San Francisco, Calif.

1991   Art and Crime (traveling exhibition), Minneapolis-St. Paul
        Bar Association, Minn.

1990   Italian Landscapes, Contemporary Realist Gallery,
        San Francisco, Calif.

        Landscape Painting 1960–1990: The Italian Tradition in
        American Art, Gibbes Museum of Art, Charleston, S.C.,
        and Bayly Art Museum, University of Virginia,
        Charlottesville, Va.

        Six Figure Painters, Contemporary Realist Gallery,
        San Francisco, Calif.

        Objects Observed: Contemporary Still-life,
        Gallery Henoch, New York, N.Y.

1988   Storytelling: Narrative Painting, New Jersey Center for
        Visual Arts, Summit, N.J.

        The Nude, One Penn Plaza, New York, N.Y.

        100th Anniversary Exhibition, Pratt Institute,
        Pratt Manhattan Gallery, N.Y.

        Joel Burger Gallery, Provincetown, Mass.

        Narrative Painting, Florida International University
        Museum, Miami, Fla.

1987   From the Nude, University of Virginia, Charlottesville, Va.

        Drawing Invitational, Indiana University Art Museum,
        Bloomington, Ind.

        Storytellers, Contemporary Realist Gallery,
        San Francisco, Calif.

        Joel Burger Gallery, Provincetown, Mass. (two person)

1986   Portraits, New York Studio School, New York, N.Y.

        Intimate and Intense: The New Genre Painting,
        Payne Gallery, Moravian College, Allentown, Pa.

        Short Stories, One Penn Plaza, New York, N.Y.

        Narrative Drawings, New York Studio School,
        New York, N.Y.

        American Still-Life Painting, Sherry French Gallery,
        New York, N.Y.

1985   Survival of the Fittest II, Ingbar Gallery, New York, N.Y.

        Psychologically Charged, Sherry French Gallery,
        New York, N.Y.

1984   Contemporary American Portrait Painting,
        Schoelkopf Gallery, New York, N.Y.

        9 Realists Revisited, Schoelkopf Gallery, New York, N.Y.

1983   American Still Life: 1945–1983 (traveling exhibition),
        Contemporary Arts Museum, Houston, Tex.

1982   Still Life/Interiors, Contemporary Arts Center,
        New Orleans, La.

        Realists Revisited, Quincy Art Center, Quincy, Ill.

1981   Contemporary American Realism Since 1960
(traveling exhibition), Pennsylvania Academy of Fine
Arts, Philadelphia, Pa.; Virginia Museum of Fine Arts,
Richmond, Va.; Oakland Museum, Oakland, Calif.;
Gulbenkian Museum, Lisbon, Portugal;
Germanische National Museum, Nuremburg, Germany

1976   The Figure as Form: American Painting 1930–1975
(traveling exhibition), Museum of Fine Arts,
St. Petersburg, Fla.

Bicentennial Landscape Painting, traveling exhibition
commissioned by U.S. Dept. of Interior,
Washington, D.C.

In Praise of Space, Westminster College,
New Wilmington, Pa.

1974   Trends in Contemporary Realist Painting, Museum of Fine
Arts, Boston, Mass.

Living American Artists and the Figure, Pennsylvania
State University, State College, Pa.

American Academy of Arts and Letters, New York, N.Y.

Contemporary Portraits by American Painters, Lowe Art
Museum, University of Miami, Miami, Fla.

1973   American Landscape, The Arts Club of Chicago,
Chicago, Ill.

1972   A Sense of Place, Sheldon Memorial Art Gallery, Lincoln,
and Joslyn Art Museum, Omaha, Neb.

Penthouse Exhibition of the Junior Council, Museum of
Modern Art, New York, N.Y.

The Realist Revisited, American Federation of Arts,
New York, N.Y.

American Academy of Arts and Letters, New York, N.Y.

The American Landscape, Boston University,
Boston, Mass.

1970   22 Realists, Whitney Museum of American Art,
New York, N.Y.

Six Figurative Artists, Indiana University Art Museum,
Bloomington, Ind.

New Jersey State Museum, Trenton, N.J. (four person)

1969   Aspects of a New Realism (traveling exhibition), Milwaukee
Art Center, Milwaukee, Wis.; Contemporary Arts
Museum, Houston, Tex.; Akron Art Institute, Akron,
Ohio.

The American Sense of Reality, Philbrook Art Center,
Tulsa, Okla.

1968   The American Landscape, Peridot Gallery, New York, N.Y.

Realism Now, Vassar College, Art Gallery,
Poughkeepsie, N.Y.

1967   Time and Place, J. Walter Thompson, New York, N.Y.

1965   Felix Landau Gallery, Los Angeles, Calif. (four person)

1964   Nine Realists, Boston University, Boston, Mass.

1963   Nine Realists, Schoelkopf Gallery, New York, N.Y.

George Lester Gallery, Rome, Italy

1962   Landscape Painting, Kornblee Gallery, New York, N.Y.

Tanager Gallery, New York, N.Y.

1960	Tanager Gallery, New York, N.Y. (three person)
1959	Brooklyn Museum of Art, Brooklyn, N.Y.
1958	Brooklyn Museum of Art, Brooklyn, N.Y.
1957	Library of Congress, Washington, D.C.
	Munson-Williams-Proctor Institute, Utica, N.Y.
	Tanager Gallery, New York, N.Y.

SELECTED COLLECTIONS

Archdiocese of Baton Rouge, La.

Art Institute of Chicago, Chicago, Ill.

Chase Manhattan Bank

Cleveland Museum of Art, Cleveland, Ohio

Davidson Collection

Edmund P. Pillsbury

Fidelity Bank, Philadelphia, Pa.

FMC Corporation, Chicago, Ill.

Glenn C. Janss Collection, Boise Art Museum, Boise, Idaho

Herbert F. Johnson Museum of Art, Cornell University, Ithaca, N.Y.

Jane Livingston

Malcolm Holzman

Mead Art Museum, Amherst College, Amherst, Mass.

Montclair State University, Montclair, N.J.

Museum of Fine Arts, Boston, Mass.

National Academy of Design, New York, N.Y.

National Gallery of Art, Washington, D.C.

National Museum (Muzium Negara), Kuala Lumpur, Malaysia

Robert Natkin

Rose Art Museum, Brandeis University, Waltham, Mass.

Sierra Club

Smithsonian American Art Museum, Washington, D.C.

Uris-Hilton Hotels

Weatherspoon Art Museum, University of North Carolina, Greensboro, N.C.

William Bailey

PUBLICATIONS AUTHORED BY GABRIEL LADERMAN

1982	"Giorgio Morandi." *Art Journal* 42 (Summer 1982): 155–56.
1971	"Unconventional Realists: Sculpture." *Artforum* 9 (March 1971): 35.
1970	"Notes from the Underground." *Artforum* 9 (Sept. 1970): 59–61.
1970	"On the Uses of the Past and of the Too-Recent Past." *Artforum* 8 (Feb. 1970): 56.
1969	"Expressionism: Concentric and Eccentric." *Artforum* 7 (Feb. 1969): 50–53.
1969	"The Outer Light." *Art News Annual* xxxv (Nov. 1969): 59–71.

1968   "The Future of Landscape Painting," *Artforum* 7
        (Nov. 1968): 57–60.

1968   "The Re-Hanging of the Met's 19th Century Galleries."
        Artforum 6 (Feb. 1968): 33–35.

1967   "Unconventional Realists," *Artforum* 6
        (Nov. 1967): 42–46.

1966   "The Importance of Cézanne." *ARTnews* 65
        (Oct. 1966): 39–41, 76–78.

1966   "Being and Becoming." *Art Journal* 25
        (Winter 1965–66): 148–49.

        Gabriel Laderman's blog: http://gabrielladerman.vox.com

Selected Bibliography

Bass, Ruth. Review at the Robert Schoelkopf Gallery. *Artforum* 11
    (Jan. 1973): 83.

_____. Review at the Robert Schoelkopf Gallery. *ARTnews* 85
    (May 1986): 135–36.

_____. Review at the Robert Schoelkopf Gallery. *ARTnews* 90
    (Jan. 1991): 152.

_____. Review at Tatistcheff & Co. *ARTnews* 93
    (Summer 1994): 178.

_____. Review at Tatistcheff & Co. *ARTnews* 97
    (Feb. 1998): 120–21.

Battcock, Gregory. *Super Realism: A Critical Anthology.* New York: E.P.
    Dutton, 1975.

Bergmann, Meredith. Exhibition Review. *The New York Review of
    Art 1* (Summer 1994).

Berlind, R. Review at the Robert Schoelkopf Gallery.
    Art in America 65 (July 1977): 100–101.

Brenson, Michael. Review at the Robert Schoelkopf Gallery.
    New York Times (Nov. 9, 1990): C32.

Campbell, Lawrence. Review at the Robert Schoelkopf Gallery.
    ARTnews 63 (Nov. 1964): 10–11.

_____. Review at the Robert Schoelkopf Gallery.
    ARTnews 66 (Nov. 1967): 12–13.

_____. Review at the Robert Schoelkopf Gallery.
    ARTnews 68 (Nov. 1969): 22.

_____. "Gabriel Laderman: A World Inside Itself."
    ARTnews 71 (Oct. 1972): 88–91.

_____. Review at the Robert Schoelkopf Gallery.
   ARTnews 73 (Sept. 1974): 114.

Canaday, John. Review at the Robert Schoelkopf Gallery.
   New York Times (Nov. 7, 1964): 24.

Carbone, David. *Gabriel Laderman*. Exhibition catalogue,
   Tatistcheff & Co., 1997.

Civitico, Bruno. "An Analysis of Recent Landscape and Narrative
   Paintings by Gabriel Laderman." *American Artist* 50
   (April 1986): 36–41.

Cochrane, Diane. "Gabriel Laderman: The Complete Artist."
   American Artist 37 (Oct. 1973): 44–49.

DeMott, Helen. Review at Tanager Gallery. *Arts Magazine* 35
   (March 1961): 56.

Esplund, Lance. "Working the Paint." *Modern Painters* 11
   (Spring 1998): 116–18.

Fairchild, Granville C. Review at the Robert Schoelkopf Gallery.
   Arts Magazine 41 (May 1967): 65.

Gibson, Eric. "American Still Life Painting." *The New Criterion*
   (Oct. 1984): 70–75.

Goodstein, Barbara. Review at the Robert Schoelkopf Gallery.
   Art & Antiques 8 (Jan. 1991): 89–90.

Gray, Don. "Gabriel Laderman, Poetic American Realist Painter,
   Robert Schoelkopf Gallery." http://www.jessieevans-dongray.com/
   essays/essay073.html (1986).

Grimes, Nancy. Review at Tatistcheff & Co. *Art in America* 82
   (July 1994): 90.

Haggerty, Gerard. Review at the Robert Schoelkopf Gallery.
   Arts Magazine 60 (March 1986): 110.

Hayes, Richard. Review at Tanager Gallery.
   ARTnews 60 (March 1961): 12.

Henry, Gerrit. Review at the Robert Schoelkopf Gallery.
   Art in America 79 (July 1991): 120–21.

_____. Exhibition Review. *Art in America* 86
   (June 1998): 108–9.

Hollander, John. "Crimes of the Art." *Art in America* 74 (April 1986):
   172–75.

Johnson, Ken. Review at Tatistcheff & Co. *New York Times* (Nov. 21, 1997): E43.

Kahn, Wolf. "Autocratic and Democratic Still-Life Painting." *American Artist* 50 (Feb. 1986): 62–69.

Kramer, Hilton. "Laderman's Conservative Ambitions." *New York Times* (April 15, 1967): 28.

_____. "Where Landscape Painting Has Gone." *New York Times* (Feb. 4, 1968): D33.

_____. "Art: Enterprise of Faith." *New York Times* (Nov. 1, 1969): 40.

Kultermann, Udo. *New Realism*. Translated from the original German publication, *Radikaler Realismus*. Greenwich, Conn.: New York Graphic Society, 1972.

Lanes, Jerrold. Review at the Robert Schoelkopf Gallery. *Artforum* 8 (Jan. 1970): 73.

Larson, Kay. "Painting the Public Lands." *ARTnews* 75 (Jan. 1976): 32–36.

Lucie-Smith, Edward. *Super Realism*. Oxford: Phaidon Press Limited, 1979.

Meyer, Susan E., ed. *20 Oil Painters and How They Work*. New York: Watson-Guptill Publications, 1978.

Perl, Jed. Review at the Robert Schoelkopf Gallery. *Arts Magazine* 51 (May 1977): 5.

_____. "The Life of the Object: Still Life Painting Today," *Arts Magazine* 52 (Dec. 1977): 124–28.

_____. "The Representational Impulse: Painting in New York 1960–1985." *The New Criterion* 3 (April 1985): 20.

_____. "Story Tellers." *The New Criterion* 4 (May 1986): 57–63.

_____. "Sex, Love and Art in the '80's." *Vogue* (May 1986): 120.

_____. "The Show Must Go On." *The New Criterion* 6 (Sept. 1987): 58.

_____. "Romance: On Gabriel Laderman, Robert Kushner and Balthus." *The New Criterion* 9 (Dec. 1990): 52–54.

_____. *Gallery Going: Four Seasons in the Art World*. New York: Harcourt Brace Jovanovich, 1991.

_____. "Selected Work from the Contemporary Realist Gallery of San Francisco: New York Academy of Art." *The New Criterion* 10 (Feb. 1992): 52.

_____. "Death and Realism." *The New Republic* 218 (April 1998): 25–30.

_____. "The Unvarnished Truth." *Modern Painters* (April 1998): 21–25.

_____. *Eye Witness: Reports from an Art World in Crisis.* New York: Basic Books, 2000.

Ratcliff, Carter. "Twenty-two Realists Exhibit at the Whitney." *Art International* 14 (April 1970): 67.

_____. Review at the Robert Schoelkopf Gallery. *Artforum* 11 (Jan. 1973): 83–84.

Roche, Harry. "Tableux Thick with Mystery." *ARTweek* 22 (April 1991): 14.

Schwartz, Sanford. Review at the Robert Schoelkopf Gallery. *Art International* 17 (Jan. 1973): 70.

Stevens, Mark. "Mark Stevens on Art: Connoisseurs of Classicism." *The New Republic* 194 (June 9, 1986): 25–28.

Tillim, Sidney. Review at the Robert Schoelkopf Gallery. *Arts Magazine* 39 (Dec. 1964): 65.

_____. "Evaluations and Re-Evaluations." *Artforum* 6 (Summer 1968): 20–23.

_____. "A Variety of Realisms." *Artforum* 7 (Summer 1969): 42.

_____. *Looking Critically: 21 Years of Artforum Magazine.* Edited by Amy Baker Sandback. Ann Arbor: UMI Research Press, 1984.

Wallin, Leland. "Toys Take a Holiday, Play the Theater, and Travel Through Time." *Arts Magazine* 61 (March 1987): 44–47.

Ward, John L. *American Realist Painting, 1945–1980.* Ann Arbor: UMI Research Press, 1989.

GABRIEL LADERMAN has served as a visiting artist and lecturer at numerous institutions, both in the United States and internationally:

American University
Amherst College
Arizona State University
Art Students League
Bennington College
Boston Art Institute
Boston University
Brooklyn College
Chautauqua Summer Art Program
Connecticut College for Women
Cornell University
Delaware School of Design
Hobart and William Smith Colleges
Indiana University
Iowa State University
Kansas City Art Institute

Long Beach State College
Louisiana State University
Maryland Institute of Art
Montclair State University
Moore College of Art
National Academy of Art and Design
New York Studio School
Ox-Bow, School of the Art Institute of Chicago
Parsons School Graduate School
Philadelphia College of Art
Princeton University
Skowhegan
Smith College
Southwest Missouri State College
Stanford University
SUNY, New Paltz
Swain School of Art
Syracuse University
Tyler School

University of Arkansas, Fayetteville
University of California, Santa Barbara
University of Florida
University of Northern Iowa
University of Pennsylvania
University of Virginia
Vassar College
Viterbo College
Wright State University
Yale University

Art Schools in Ballarat, Victoria, Australia
Prahran University, Melbourne, Australia
Royal Art School, Bangkok, Thailand
USIS Japan Lectures in Nagasaki, Nagoya, Tokyo, and Sapporo
USIS Indonesia Lectures in Jogjakarta and Surabaya
Victorian College of Art, Melbourne, Australia

PHOTO CREDITS

Mixed Sources
Product group from well-managed
forests and other controlled sources
www.fsc.org Cert no. BV-COC-080420
© 1996 Forest Stewardship Council

Printed by Capital Offset Company, Inc., Concord,
New Hampshire, on PhoeniXmotion Xenon Dull.